Wildlife in Britain

Part One

Stephen Moss

This edition produced exclusively for The Daily Telegraph 2009 from
THE BUMPER BOOK OF NATURE
By Stephen Moss
Published by Square Peg

First published in Great Britain in 2009 by
Square Peg
Random House, 20 Vauxhall Bridge Road,
London SW1V 2SA

The Random House Group Limited Reg. No. 954009

www.rbooks.co.uk/thebumperbookofnature

ISBN 9780224086431

While every effort has been made to ensure the accuracy of the information contained in this book, in
no circumstances can the publisher or the author accept any legal responsibility or liability for any loss or
damage (including damage to property and/or personal injury) arising from any error or omission from
the information contained in this book, or from the failure of the reader to properly and accurately follow
any instructions contained in the book. This book contains a number of activities which may be dangerous
if you do not follow the instructions given. For children under the age of 18, these activities should be
supervised by an adult.

Contents

Introduction

When you think back to your own childhood, what do you remember? Did you climb trees, build dens, and fish for tiddlers? Of course you did — that's how we entertained ourselves in the days before computer games and a TV in every room.

To stave off boredom, we begged our parents to let us go and play outside. Ball games in the street were just the start — soon we were scrambling over the fence and into the woods, exploring nature for ourselves.

So what can we all do to get back in touch with nature? Well, for a start, I hope you will use these extracts from *The Bumper Book of Nature* — and those in tomorrow's *Sunday Telegraph* — to get out and experience the wonders of the natural world for yourselves. There are things you can do in any back garden, or local park — on your own or as a family. And to help you identify the animals and plants you see, there are identification guides, beautifully illustrated by some of Britain's finest wildlife artists.

Stephen Moss

Become a bat detective

There are seventeen different kinds of bat in Britain — over one-quarter of all our mammal species — yet apart from the occasional glimpse at dusk on a warm summer's evening, we hardly ever see them. That's because they spend the daylight hours roosting in the attics of houses, old barns or caves, and only emerge at night to hunt for their insect prey.

Some people are put off by all the folklore about bats, so let's get a few things straight. Apart from South American vampire bats, they don't suck blood; they don't get tangled in your hair; and bats are most certainly not blind. In fact they have pretty good eyesight, although they track down their prey using a very different technique.

Bats hunt by 'echo-location' — uttering a series of rapid clicks which 'bounce off' any objects in the air. By listening to the echo made when the sound hits the object, the bat knows how close it is, even if it can't actually see it.

Bats also know whether what they are hearing is made by a solid object like a wall, or a moving prey item like a moth – enabling them either to avoid a collision or to catch their dinner.

If you want to learn more about bats, the best way is to go on an organised bat walk. These usually take place at dusk during the spring and summer, and are run by local bat groups and wildlife trusts.

Because bats call at very high frequencies – generally too high for the human ear to detect – the group leader will usually bring a 'bat detector'. This clever instrument can convert the calls into a series of clicks which we are then able to hear.

Different kinds of bats call at different sound frequencies; some bats have very rhythmic calls, and others warble, almost like a bird. So an experienced 'bat-man' or 'bat-woman' will be able to identify the particular species you are hearing.

On some bat walks, especially later in the year, the leader may look inside bat nesting boxes and bring out a bat for you to look at. You'll be amazed at how tiny they are, with such delicate wings – yet the bat is a really impressive flyer, rivalling even the birds with its aerobatic skills.

The smallest British bats, the pipistrelles, are about three centimetres long and weigh as little as four grams – about the same as a two-pence coin. The largest, the noctule, has a wingspan of 30–40 centimetres and weighs about 25–40 grams – about the same as a house sparrow.

Go on a city safari

Cities are often known as 'urban jungles' – and you might think that this would mean wild creatures would struggle to find a home there. But far from being tough, hostile environments for wildlife, they in fact provide everything the creature-about-town needs.

Whether a wild creature is looking for food, water, shelter, light or heat, the modern city provides it. As a result, a whole host of animals — and plants — have moved lock, stock and barrel into our urban areas.

They're not just surviving there, but thriving. Every single major animal group — from birds of prey to deer, and from seabirds to seals — can be found in at least one British city. And because these animals have got used to living alongside millions of us, they are often far less wary than their country cousins.

Take the urban fox. In the countryside, where until recently they have been hunted, foxes are shy creatures, rarely seen apart from a bushy red tail disappearing out of sight. Yet in our towns and cities they will stroll down the street without a care in the world — knowing that as long as they can avoid the traffic, they are safe.

One of the best ways to get to know the wildlife of a town or city is to treat it just like any other place to watch wildlife — and go on an urban safari. By planning your route so it takes in a range of different locations and habitats, you should not only see a wide range of plants and animals, but get great views as well.

Tips

- Get hold of a really detailed map – the Ordnance Survey Pathfinder range (1:25,000 scale or 4cm to 1km) is ideal.
- Plan your route – try to include a patch of woodland, the local park, a river or canal – as each new habitat is likely to bring new sightings.
- Take a pair of binoculars, a couple of field guides and a notebook to write down what you see.
- As always, a digital camera is a good way to record sightings (especially plants and insects) for you to identify later, when you get home.
- Don't forget to look down – cities, and especially ports like London, Liverpool and Bristol, have all sorts of exotic foreign plants growing in some unlikely places.

Classic city locations and what to look for

- London: red and fallow deer and ring-necked parakeets in Richmond Park; stag beetles on Wimbledon Common; peregrines on Tate Modern; cormorants, herons and swans on the Thames; water voles, bats and birdlife at the London Wetland Centre.
- Birmingham: kingfishers on the canal network.
- Glasgow: foxes in the suburbs of the West End.
- Brighton: huge winter roost of starlings on the Palace Pier.
- Dundee: red squirrels in the city parks.
- Newcastle: nesting kittiwakes on the Tyne Bridge; seals and the occasional otter in the Tyne.
- Bristol: peregrines and buzzards over Avon Gorge.
- Manchester: peregrines on the Arndale Shopping centre.
- Cardiff: salmon leaping on the River Taff.

Listen for woodpeckers drumming

On a warm, fine day in February or March, listen out for the drumming of woodpeckers. The best places to hear them are woods with plenty of large, old trees.

Male woodpeckers drum to defend their territory against rival males, and to attract a mate. By far the most frequent drummer is the great spotted, though green and the rare lesser spotted woodpeckers also drum.

From early spring onwards, the male selects a suitable tree (usually a hollow branch or trunk of a dead or dying one), and then proceeds to drum – producing up to forty blows every second.

You might think that woodpeckers would get a headache from banging their beak against a tree – the equivalent of you or me repeatedly hitting our head against a wall at 26km per hour – but in fact they are superbly adapted to do so.

Woodpeckers have a thick skull, and their brains are very tightly packed inside to reduce the effects of shaking. They also have spongy tissue around their beak which acts like a car's shock absorbers. The eyes are carefully protected, and are closed just before the beak hits the tree to avoid being damaged by flying bits of bark.

Once you've heard the woodpecker drumming, the next step is to try to see it. Woodpeckers are shy birds, and their drumming can carry a long way, so approach slowly and quietly, until you're sure you're close to the drumming tree.

Then, taking a stick, beat a rapid rhythm on the tree trunk, trying to reproduce the woodpecker's own sound. With luck the bird will stop drumming and come to investigate what he thinks is a rival male intruding into his territory.

Once you've had a good view, don't confuse the poor chap by beating the stick again, as he needs to get back to drumming to keep hold of his territory.

How to identify ...
large mammals

Britain's larger mammals include some of our commonest and most familiar animals, as well as some of the rarest and most difficult to see. In the first group are the rabbit, fox and badger; while even the keenest mammal enthusiasts struggle to see polecats, pine martens and the elusive Scottish wild cat.

After suffering at the hands of hunting and pollution, some creatures, such as the otter, are making a comeback. Meanwhile, one of our favourite mammals, the red squirrel, continues to decline as a result of competition with the greys introduced from North America.

As well as land-based mammals, don't forget the two species of seal, both of which can be easily seen at special sites around our coasts. Land-based mammals (e.g. deer) live excusively on land; the term 'resident mammals' includes all land mammals and coastal marine mammals which breed on land (e.g. seals), but not whales.

How to identify ...
large mammals

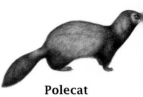

Rabbit

The classic bunny of children's stories is not a native British species at all, but was brought here by Norman invaders for food. It is found all over lowland Britain – living together in networks of tunnels known as warrens. Best time to see them is in late afternoon on a warm summer's day when the youngsters are out playing.

Polecat

The ancestor of the domestic ferret, and very similar in appearance: with a dark body and paler belly, and a distinctive masked face pattern. Nocturnal, and very hard to see.

Stoat

The stoat is a lean, mean, killing machine – pound for pound our most voracious predator, and able to kill a rabbit many times its own weight. Larger and bulkier than the weasel, with a black tip to its tail. In hilly regions turns white in winter – known as 'ermine'.

Brown Hare

Larger than the rabbit, with much longer, black-tipped ears, and very long hind legs, enabling it to run very fast. Hares do not use burrows – instead, when frightened, they'll crouch low into a hollow known as a 'form'. In spring, watch out for 'mad March hares' boxing – as females test out rival males.

Mountain Hare

Slightly smaller relative of the brown hare, found in hilly and mountainous regions of Scotland, Ireland and the Peak District in England. In winter, the mountain hare's coat turns white.

Otter

This beautiful creature has made a comeback in recent years and is now found in rivers and waterways throughout Britain – even in some cities. Large, sleek and equally suited to water or land. Otters are often nocturnal, but on Scottish coasts may be seen at any time of day, as their lifestyle is governed by the tides.

North American Mink

An introduced mammal which has wreaked havoc on our native animals such as the water vole. Smaller and darker than the otter, and also found in rivers, streams and other waterways. May now be declining as a result of the otter's comeback.

Weasel

Smaller than the closely related stoat – a long, slender creature usually seen briefly as it dashes across a road or path before disappearing into a grassy verge. If you get good views, look out for the tail, which lacks the stoat's black tip.

Pine Marten

This beautiful creature can be found in parts of Scotland and Ireland, and although very shy has been known to come to bird tables to feed. Chestnut brown above and buff below, with a long body and tail.

Red Squirrel

Britain's native squirrel has suffered major declines in numbers and range during the last century, and is now only found in Scotland, Ireland, parts of northern England and Wales, and a few outposts in southern England.

Grey Squirrel

Not the most popular British mammal, and not really British, but introduced from North America over a hundred years ago.

Wild Cat

Only found in Scotland, one of our rarest and most elusive large mammals — almost impossible to see.

Badger

The legendary 'brock' is one of our easiest mammals to recognise — with its dark grey body, stocky appearance and black-and-white face pattern. Common and widespread, but because of its nocturnal habits not always easy to see.

Fox

This originally rural, shy animal is nowadays most likely to be seen in our towns and cities, roaming the urban jungle and scavenging for food from dustbins. Our only wild dog, easily recognised by its reddish-brown coat.

Common Seal

Smaller and more friendly-looking than the grey seal — and actually less common — with a doglike facial expression. Comes in variety of colours, and found around our coasts, especially in Scotland.

Wild Boar

This ancient forest dweller went extinct in Britain centuries ago, but has made a comeback after escaping from farms in parts of southern Britain.

Grey Seal

Our largest resident mammal, and the larger and commoner of our two species of seal. Told apart from common seal by more haughty appearance with massive nose. Found around our coasts, especially in the north and west.

Identify different birdsong

Getting to know songs and calls is a bit like learning a foreign language — apparently impossible at first, daunting, and often confusing. No wonder so many people give up at the first hurdle, or don't even bother to start.

But unless you know at least a few sounds of common birds you will miss out on so much — most experienced birders identify at least half the birds they hear on song or call — especially in spring, when birdsong is at its peak.

So here are a few tips on learning the sounds of our common birds — plus some useful mnemonics or memory aids to help you. Hopefully, you'll find that, just like learning a foreign language, once you have mastered the basics things get a bit easier — and a lot more rewarding.

Tips

- Start in February or March when the resident species are in full song, but before the summer migrants have returned — it's less confusing that way.
- Get outdoors early in the day — birds sing most just before and after sunrise.
- Go to the right place: a local park or woodland will be the most productive, but your garden is also a good place to start as you can practise every day.
- Avoid areas with lots of noise from traffic or people.
- Listen first, and then try to track down the bird that's singing and put a name to it.
- Concentrate on three elements — pitch, rhythm and tone:
  - Pitch: is it high or low?
  - Rhythm: fast or slow? Continuous or broken up into phrases? Repetitive or unpredictable?
  - Tone: is it happy or sad? Harsh or musical?

Some useful memory aids

- Great tit: sings a rhythmic song on two notes – 'tea-cher, tea-cher, tea-cher ...'
- Blue tit: a rather unexciting series of high-pitched notes – 'see-see-see-see-see ...'
- Robin: sweet, plaintive song delivered in short, apparently random phrases.
- Blackbird: much deeper and fruitier than other birds; also in short, deliberate phrases.
- Song thrush: repeats every phrase several times, using two or three notes at a time – 'Get up, get up, get up; go to bed, go to bed, go to bed ...'
- Wren: delivers an astonishingly loud series of phrases with trills and whistles, ending on a flourishing trill.
- Dunnock: a rather odd little song which doesn't seem to have a definite start or end.
- Starling: bizarre series of whistles and metallic tones – more like a machine than a bird; may also mimic anything from car alarms to mobile phone tones.
- House sparrow: an unassuming series of chirps; not really a song as such.
- Pied wagtail: loud, two-note call as it flies off – sounds like 'Chis-ick!'
- Chaffinch: a series of notes descending the scale and speeding up towards the end – has been compared to a cricketer running up to deliver a fast ball.
- Goldfinch: like tinkling bells – very pleasing to the ear.
- Greenfinch: full of harsh, metallic sounds – not very pleasing to the ear.
- Chiffchaff: sings its own name in short phrases – 'chiff-chiff-chaff-chiff-chaff ...'

Find a bird's nest

Egg-collecting is now against the law, and for very good reason. Birds have enough problems to deal with in the breeding season without having to lay their clutch of eggs again because someone has raided their nest.

Finding birds' nests is not as easy as it sounds – most are hidden away in dense vegetation, to stop predators finding the precious eggs or chicks – and learning how to spot them gave many older birdwatchers a really good apprenticeship in getting to know various different species.

There is nothing wrong with looking for nests, just don't disturb the occupants. Here are some tips on what to look for, when and how.

Timing

- Most birds breed in spring – though in the bird world that can start as early as January (and possibly before Christmas during mild winters) and go on into late summer or even autumn.
- The best time to look for nests is March or April.
- Some birds don't come back from Africa until April or May – so don't look for swallow or house martin nests too early.

Where to look

- Keep your eyes open when you're on a walk. Look at different levels – some birds like robins and wrens nest very low down in vegetation like brambles; others, like crows and magpies, nest high in the top of a tree.
- Some nests are really obvious, such as those built by rooks – in a colony high in tall trees known as a 'rookery'. Rooks start nesting in February, and until the trees come into leaf you can easily find and watch them.

continues on page 18

How to identify …

garden birds

If you want to learn how to identify birds, then your garden is a great place to start. Put up a bird table and some feeders and you'll soon be able to take a good look at the birds that visit — and get to know the differences between them.

You probably already know more than you think. Most people can notice the difference between a song thrush and a blackbird, or tell a house sparrow apart from a starling. Robins are easy, and with practice, you'll soon be sorting out the various tits and finches that come to your feeders.

Use the illustrations here as a guide to get you started, but if you're not sure what a bird is, then check it out in a proper bird book to make sure.

How to identify ...
garden birds

Pied Wagtail
Delightful little black-and-white bird with a long tail, usually seen walking around on the lawn, driveway or pavement, picking up tiny insects with its long, pointed bill.

Wood Pigeon
Large, plump pigeon with grey back, pinkish breast and obvious white ring around its neck. Five-syllable call, sounds like 'my toe is bleeding'!

Collared Dove
Smaller and more delicate than Wood Pigeon. Mainly pinkish buff, with a black collar around the neck. Three-syllable call, sounds like 'U-ni-ted, u-ni-ted'!

Dunnock
An unassuming little bird: robin-shaped but with markings similar to a sparrow – hence its old name of 'hedge sparrow'. Look for the long, pointed bill and greyish-mauve head and neck.

Wren
One of our smallest birds – and the commonest in Britain – but quite shy and retiring, so it's easy to miss. Look for a tiny brown bird with a short, cocked tail. And in spring, listen for the wren's loud, trilling song.

Great Spotted Woodpecker
Smart, starling-sized, black-and-white woodpecker with bright crimson patch under the tail, and with the male, on the back of the head. May come to bird feeders, but quite shy.

Robin
Adults unmistakable: brown above with orange-red breast and pale belly. Youngsters lack the red breast and are spotty, but have the same plump shape and beady eye as their parents.

Blackbird
Male easy to identify, with his all-black plumage, beady eye and bright custard-yellow bill. Females and youngsters are brown, but plain (not spotted like the thrushes).

Song Thrush
The classic thrush, with a spotty breast and chocolate-brown upperparts. The scarcer mistle thrush is much larger, paler and greyer, and has a less 'friendly' expression.

Blue Tit
A garden favourite: tiny, active and always looking for trouble. Blue head and back contrasts with white cheeks and yellow underneath. Loves seed and nut feeders and nest boxes.

Great Tit
Larger than blue tit, with no blue in the plumage at all. Look out for the black head contrasting with white cheeks, moss-green back, and yellow underparts with a thick black line running down the middle.

Starling
Often ignored, Starlings deserve a closer look. Their plumage shines with glossy greens and purples (especially in summer), while in winter they are covered in tiny white spots. Check out the base of the yellow bill: blue for a male, pink for a female.

Jay
A shy relative of the magpie, with a stunning pink plumage, streaky crest, black bill, wings and tail, and a bright blue patch on its wings.

Magpie
The classic pantomime villain of the garden: this noisy, brash black-and-white bird is actually a real beauty, with subtle greens and purples in its plumage, which are easiest to see when the sun shines.

Jackdaw
Our smallest crow, mainly black apart from a light grey patch on the back of its neck. Short, stubby bill. Sociable, and often seen in noisy flocks.

Goldfinch
Beautiful little finch, with a crimson face patch, black-and-white head pattern, and black wings with a golden-yellow stripe which is even more obvious when they fly. Sharp beak for feeding on tiny seeds. Usually seen in flocks.

Greenfinch
Males easy to spot, with their moss-green plumage and yellow in the wing. Females and youngsters can be confused with sparrows, but always show some yellow or green colour in their feathers.

Chaffinch
The male is one of our handsomest birds: pink below, with a grey head and two bright white wing bars. Female looks a bit like a female sparrow, but has cleaner plumage and white wing bars.

House Sparrow
Sociable, cheeky little bird, usually seen in a group. Males have a black bib, grey head, pale grey cheeks and brown back. Females are duller brown; plain beneath and streaky above.

- Other really obvious nests are those made by house martins built on the side of a house, just beneath the eaves. In May you can watch house martins build (or rebuild) their nests using tiny balls of mud.

What to look for

- Not all nests are the same size and shape. Some, like those made by small birds such as thrushes and robins, are neat, cup-shaped structures lined with grass or mud. Others, like that of the magpie, are a rough assembly of sticks in the branches or twigs of a tree.
- Many birds, including tits and woodpeckers, nest out of sight in holes in trees – where they and their eggs and chicks can be safe from predators. Although you can't see the nest itself, you can sit and watch the birds flying in and out.
- Some birds – especially robins, pied wagtails and blackbirds – often make their nests in really unusual places. Odd nest sites have included a teapot, under the bonnet of a working Land Rover, the coat pocket of a gardener (while he had hung it up in his tool shed between breakfast and lunch) and even (a long time ago) in the skull of a hanged man.

How to find a nest

- By far the best way to find a nest – and to learn more about the bird and its habits – is to sit quietly in a suitable spot and watch the behaviour of the birds you see.
- Look out for birds carrying nesting material such as grass, leaves or twigs (early in the season) or food for chicks (later on).
- Parent birds will also remove the chicks' droppings in a 'faecal sac' – memorably described by Bill Oddie as 'shrink-wrapped poo'.

continues on page 22

How to identify ...

frogs, toads and newts

Britain's tally of amphibians is not very impressive: just nine species, three of which were introduced from abroad. Of these, there are four species of frog, two kinds of toad and three types of newt. All breed in water, but spend much of their life cycle on land – characteristic of all the world's 5,700 or so amphibian species.

And just like amphibians everywhere, Britain's frogs, toads and newts are under threat. The main problem is loss of habitat – the number of ponds in Britain has fallen dramatically in the past fifty years or so, as more and more wetlands are drained for farming, or to build homes or roads. Disease is another problem, as is pollution. So if you do come across any amphibians, make sure you don't disturb them – they need all the help they can get.

frogs, toads and newts

Common Frog

The most familiar British amphibian is also one of the most threatened – in fact, it only survives in some areas thanks to garden ponds, which provide a welcome refuge for the frogs to lay their spawn in early spring. Can vary in colour: but usually a combination of green, brown or yellow marked with dark blotches, including a distinctive mask across the eyes. Moves by hopping, using its powerful hind legs.

Edible Frog, Pool Frog and Marsh Frog

These species were all introduced from Continental Europe during the twentieth century, and are now thriving in many parts of south-east England – perhaps as a result of climate change. They are very similar-looking bright green frogs, generally detected by their incredibly loud and far-carrying calls, especially in the breeding season.

Common Toad

Although superficially similar in size and shape, toads can easily be told apart from frog by their warty skin, darker colour and habit of walking instead of hopping. Will make long journeys to get to their breeding grounds, often crossing roads or paths, where they can easily fall victim to passing traffic.

Natterjack Toad

This rare relative of the Common Toad is confined to a few sandy heaths in southern England and parts of the north-west. Best told apart from its commoner relative by the distinctive yellow stripe down the centre of its back. Can often be heard calling at night.

Great Crested Newt

The largest and rarcest British newt, he male is a magnificent creature, with a jagged crest along the length of his back and a bright orange belly. Females re less obvious, but till brightly coloured.

Smooth and Palmate Newts

These two newts are not easy to tell apart, especially outside the breeding season. Both are smaller and less well marked than the great crested, though breeding males can show an orange belly and appear quite brightly coloured.

Looking for nests on water

- Waterbirds such as ducks, swans, grebes, coots and moorhens often build their nest in full view, a few feet out into the water. To stop it floating away they attach it to an underwater plant.
- If the nest is close enough to the bank you should be able to see the eggs, and when the chicks hatch you can watch them being fed by their parents.
- The chicks of most waterbirds are 'precocial', which means they are able to swim – and to some extent fend for themselves – almost as soon as they hatch. Listen for the sound of tweeting as they anxiously call to remind their mum and dad that they're still here ...

How you can help

- If you do find a bird's nest, be careful not to disturb it. Put any foliage you've moved back into position, and move away as quickly as possible so as not to attract the attention of predators or upset the parent birds.
- In spring, put out hair (of pets, horses or humans) or bits of wool, straw and grasses for the birds to use to line their nest.
- Make a nest box.
- Put out live food such as mealworms to help parent birds feed their hungry young – especially in wet weather when they need all the help they can get.

How to identify …
dragonflies
and damselflies

These stunning creatures can sometimes be quite challenging to identify, but using a combination of clues you should be able to work most of them out. Useful clues are:

- Shape: if it holds its wings out when perched, it's a dragonfly; if it folds them along the length of its body, it's a damselfly.
- Location: check out if the insect you think you're watching lives in this particular part of the country.
- Habitat: some dragonflies prefer specialist habitats such as heathland; others can be found anywhere with water — or even some distance away.
- Timing: different dragonflies come out at different times of year — again, check this out in a field guide.
- Size: sometimes hard to judge, but with practice you'll know if you're looking at a large hawker or a smaller darter; skimmers and chasers are somewhere in between.
- Colour and pattern: pay special attention to the head and thorax (chunky part of the body), the abdomen (the long part of the body) and the wings; also look for spots (or no spots!) on the wings.
- Habits: some dragonflies are brash and bold, flying over to check you out; others are shy and wary. Some fly almost constantly; others prefer to bask in the sunshine on a leaf or path.

How to identify ...
dragonflies and damselflies

Emperor

Our largest dragonfly and one of our largest insects. Males are blue on the abdomen and green on the head and thorax; females mainly green. Found in southern Britain from June to August.

Southern Hawker

Another huge dragonfly: mainly green and brown but with blue near the end of the abdomen. Found in England, Wales and lowland Scotland from July to September. Often flies right up to you to take a close look.

Brown Hawker

The only large dragonfly with yellowish-brown wings, and a brown body with odd spots of blue. Found in southern Britain, and one of the latest to appear, from August to October.

Migrant and Common Hawkers

Two very similar medium-to-large dragon-flies: brown with blue and yellow markings. Common found more in the north, migrant in the south, from July to October.

Hairy Dragonfly
Mainly brown with blue and green markings. By far the earliest large dragonfly to appear, from late April to June, mostly in the south and east.

Four-spotted Chaser
A medium-sized, chunky dragonfly with two spots on each wing (making eight in all). Males mainly brown, females more yellow orange. Found throughout Britain from May to July.

Broad-bodied Chaser
Another chunky, medium-sized dragonfly – males are powder blue on the abdomen, females yellowish brown. Found in southern Britain from June to July.

Banded Demoiselle
A large damselfly, with delicately barred wings and a slender blue (male) or green (female) abdomen. Appears in large numbers in southern Britain from May to August.

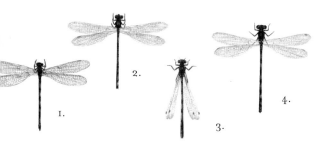

Damselflies
Several species of damselfly emerge on sunny days from late April through to August, including:

1. Common Blue, Azure and Variable: patterned bright blue and black and very hard to tell apart.
2. Blue-tailed: dark abdomen with a bright blue tip.
3. Large Red: reddish abdomen with black markings.
4. Red-eyed: dark abdomen with a blue tip and large red eyes.

Common Darter
Small dragonfly; males are reddish brown, females yellow; spots on wings. Found across most of Britain from July to October – sometimes even later in the warmer south.

Some recipes for spring flowers and plants

When I was a teenager, the naturalist Richard Mabey wrote a book called *Food for Free*, describing all the different ways to get a free meal from the countryside. I can still remember the excitement of realising that all this wonderful food was out there – just waiting to be picked …

Unfortunately the idea of collecting, cooking and eating wild plants and other natural things like fungi has pretty much gone out of fashion – buying it from the local supermarket seems so much easier. People are also worried – unduly I think – about the risk of poisoning themselves.

Of course you need to take care and make sure that you know what you're eating. But it's well worth it for the thrill of knowing that you've gone out and foraged for yourself.

Here are a few suggestions for spring food for free:

- Wild garlic: use the flowers or young leaves to add a pungent flavour to salads, or as a garnish on soup. You can even make wild-garlic bread.
- Hawthorn: hawthorn leaves can be added to salads or cheese sandwiches, or just munched as you go along on a country walk. The very early bright green buds have a wonderful nutty flavour, and the later darker green leaves taste a bit like parsley.
- Stinging nettles: young shoots picked between March and May can be prepared in the same way as spinach or similar greens or made into a tasty and nutritious soup – with lots of iron and as much vitamin C as spinach. But wear gloves to pick them – they sting until they've been cooked.
- Wild sorrel: this slightly bitter herb adds a lemony flavour to cooking, and goes well with fish dishes.

How to identify …
wayside and woodland flowers

The phrase 'wayside and woodland' may be an old-fashioned one, but it perfectly describes the kind of flowers we come across on country walks: along the sides of lanes, amongst hedgerows, and in the woods themselves. Many of these are amongst the earliest wild flowers to appear, as they need to bloom before the growth of leaves on the trees makes it too dark for them. So look out for them on country walks anytime from February onwards …

How to identify ...
wayside and
woodland flowers

Lesser Celandine

An early flower, its attractive yellow blooms bring a welcome splash of colour to our woods from February to May. Only opens when the sun shines.

Snowdrop

The first flower to appear, often before the snow has finally melted, this beautiful little plant blooms from January to March, its delicate white flowers drooping from their stems on the woodland floor.

Primrose

The original 'prima rosa', or first flower: the familiar lemon-yellow flowers appear on forest floors and along hedgerows from February to May.

Wood Anemone

Carpets of these little white flowers with their yellow centre cover the forest floor from March to May.

Wild Daffodil

Classic trumpet-shaped, pale yellow flowers with the deeper yellow centre that so inspired the poet Wordsworth. Now only found in scattered sites around the country, as competition from cultivated plants has reduced their range.

Wild Garlic (Ramsons)

The smell of wild garlic one of the classic signs spring in our woodland Clusters of spiky white flowers carpet the grou from April to May.

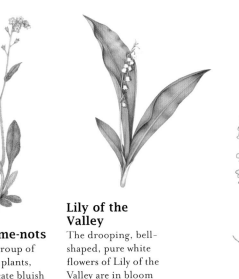

Bluebell

Our favourite wild flower, and justly so. The delicate purplish-blue flowers appear from April into June, depending on location, and produce one of our greatest natural spectacles.

Foxglove

One of our best-known and loveliest plants, growing in open woodland and moorland from June to September. Very tall, with a single spike covered with bell-shaped purple or pink flowers.

Violets

A range of closely related wild flowers, appearing from March to May on woodland floors, especially where there is a mixture of dappled sunshine and shade. Range in colour from almost blue to a delicate purple.

Forget-me-nots

Another group of woodland plants, their delicate bluish flowers with yellow centres appearing from spring through to early autumn.

Lily of the Valley

The drooping, bell-shaped, pure white flowers of Lily of the Valley are in bloom from May to June, usually in dry woodland on chalky soils.

Bird's-nest Orchid

This peculiar member of the orchid family obtains all its energy from fungi beneath the soil, and is one of the few plants able to grow in beech woods where sunlight rarely reaches the ground in summer. A single shoot protrudes from the ground, with brownish-yellow flowers.

Find the first spring flowers

What better way to welcome the coming of spring than to take a walk through your local wood and look for the very first wild flowers of the season?

Exactly when you should do this depends on where you are: spring moves up the country gradually from the south and west, so the further north and east you live, the later it will arrive in your neck of the woods. Local climate can make a difference too: plants on high ground come into bloom several weeks later than those in the valleys.

The first flowers usually appear some time in February, though the recent run of very mild winters means that in more sheltered parts of Britain they may be in bloom for the whole of the winter.

The earliest flower – the snowdrop – often appears at the end of January, and has long been associated with the Christian festival of Candlemas, which occurs on 2 February each year. The link with the Church may have come about because snowdrops often bloom in sheltered churchyards before they appear in the woods.

Another early flower is the crocus – many of these have escaped from gardens, so you shouldn't really think of them as 'wild' flowers. They still gladden the heart on a sunny day in February, though.

Of our truly wild flowers, lesser celandine has always been among the first to appear. The eighteenth-century naturalist Gilbert White gave 21 February as its usual first date, though again this pretty yellow flower may bloom later the further north you live.

Like many woodland flowers, lesser celandines need to bloom early to make the most of the sunshine, as by April or May the tree canopy has closed, and little or no sunlight reaches the forest floor.

During the last week of March, other woodland flowers are also at their best. Carpets of white wood anemones cover the ground – and if you take a closer look at their undersides you can see a lovely pinkish-purple tinge on the petals where they meet the stem. And

As spring truly arrives, wild daffodils add a splash of yellow, and the smell of ramsons — wild garlic — hangs in the air.

Although it is sometimes frowned upon, there is no harm in picking a small posy of these early-spring flowers to take home and remind you of your walk in the woods — but never dig up a plant by its roots or pick too many flowers.

Flowers which should open on certain saints' days — a list from Richard Inwards' 'Weather Lore' (1893)

2 February: Candlemas	snowdrop
14 February: St Valentine	crocus
25 March: Lady Day	daffodil
23 April: St George	harebell
3 May: Holy Cross	crowfoot
11 June: St Barnabas	ragged robin
24 June: St John the Baptist	scarlet lychnis
15 July: St Swithun	lily
20 July: St Margaret	poppy
22 July: St Mary Magdalene	rose
1 August: Lammas	camomile
15 August: Assumption	virgin's bower
24 August: St Bartholomew	sunflower
14 September: Holyrood	passion flower
29 September: Michaelmas	Michaelmas daisy
25 November: St Catherine	laurel
25 December: Christmas	ivy & holly

Look for spiders in your house

Autumn is a very good time to look for spiders — or a very bad time if you're scared of them!

One of our largest spiders, the fearsome, black Tegenaria or house spider, becomes a lot more noticeable in late summer and autumn when the males start to go walkabout to look for females to mate with.

At this time of year they can turn up anywhere in the house. But it's a myth that spiders crawl up the plug-hole — once they've fallen in, they can't climb up the slippery sides without a helping hand from us.

Another spider found in many of our homes is the daddy-long-legs spider. It's called that because it looks just like the insect known as the 'daddy-long-legs' (also called the crane fly). This unobtrusive creature sits quite still in an untidy web in the corner of the room, where the ceiling meets the wall. Until you take a closer look, you will probably think the web is empty, as the spider that lives there is so weedy it's very hard to spot.

But take a pencil, give the web a gentle prod, and the spider suddenly starts to vibrate rapidly up and down — its way of fooling other spiders which might make a meal of it. The spider will also use its long legs to throw strands of web at the intruder to fend it off.

By sitting so quietly the daddy-long-legs spider catches many an unwary insect; and will eat other spiders, including its own kind. The offspring keep out of each other's way too, for fear that they might be munched by a sibling.

The daddy-long-legs spider is not native to Britain — it originated in mainland Europe. But it has spread throughout southern England and as far north as Yorkshire by one simple method: it makes its web in pieces of furniture like wardrobes, which are then loaded into removal vans and driven around the country.

How to identify ...
butterflies

Butterflies are some of our most beautiful and fascinating insects. Their life cycle, in which an egg hatches into a caterpillar, then turns itself into a chrysalis and finally emerges as a winged adult, is little short of a miracle.

They are also common (though sadly not as common as they used to be) and easy to spot – though on fine summer's days they do fly a bit too fast to get a really close look.

There are around sixty different kinds of butterfly in Britain, of which about two-thirds are either very scarce or found only in specialised habitats such as ancient woodlands, chalk grasslands and mountainsides. But about twenty butterflies are common and widespread, and likely to be seen either in your garden, or on a walk alongside a hedgerow or at the edge of a wood. Here's a guide to telling them apart.

Different butterflies come out at different times of the year – so if you're not sure what you're looking at, check when it's most likely to be found.

How to identify ...
butterflies

Small Tortoiseshell
March to October, almost anywhere
One of our most common butterflies, can be seen in almost every month as it hibernates here. Medium-sized, with classic 'tortoiseshell' pattern of orange and black, and blue spots on the edges of the wings.

Comma
February/March to early autumn, England and Wales
Distinctive orange-and-black butterfly with crinkly edges to its wings and a tiny white mark below that gives the comma its name. Loves buddleias.

Red Admiral
April/May to September/ October, almost anywhere
One of our largest and most handsome butterflies: basically black and orange-red with white markings near the wing tips. Loves feeding on fallen fruit. Comes here each spring from Continental Europe, migrating back in autumn.

Painted Lady
May/June to August/ September, mainly in south
Like a washed-out version of the red admiral, this is another migrant, some flying here all the way from North Africa. Common in some summers; very scarce in others. Look out for a black-and-orange butterfly with white on the wing tips, and long wings.

Peacock
March/April to September, almost anywhere apart from northern Scotland Stunning creature, with huge 'eyes' on the tips of the wings which are meant to fool predators and allow the butterfly to escape from attack. Deep orange, with blue, yellow and black 'eyes'.

Marbled White
Late June to August, mainly in the south and west
Not a 'white' at all, but a 'brown' with white mottling on its dark wings. A grassland species some-times found in gardens.

'Cabbage' White
April/May to August/September, almost anywhere
This is in fact three separate but very similar species: large, small and green-veined whites. All are white above, with black spots and black edges to their wings; and yellowish below. Look out for the green-veined white's distinctive underwing pattern of black streaks on a yellow background.

Gatekeeper
July to August,
grassy areas in the south
Appears later than
the meadow brown,
and is smaller,
brighter and smarter
than that species. The
orange patches above
are more obvious
than on the meadow
brown, and the
underwings are also
brighter. 'Eyes' above
and below.

Meadow Brown
May to August/September,
almost anywhere
Our commonest and
most widespread
butterfly, but often
overlooked because of
its rather drab
appearance. Males are
basically dark brown,
with small brown
'eyes' above and
below, and orange on
the underwings.
Females have orange
on the upperwings
too. Larger than the
similar gatekeeper.
Prefers long grass.

Clouded Yellow
May to September, mainly
in the south
Another migrant,
seen in huge numbers
in some summers,
and other years virtu-
ally absent. Resembles
the brimstone, but
much deeper, richer
yellow and with
black wing tips.

Brimstone
February/March to late
autumn, mainly in England
One of the first
butterflies to emerge,
sometimes seen on
sunny days in late
winter, this is the
original 'butter-
coloured fly'. Male is
pale lemon yellow;
the female is much
paler, and can be
confused with one of
the 'whites', but has
no black on her
wings.

Orange Tip
April to June, almost
anywhere
The male is really easy
to spot, thanks to the
bright orange patches
on his white wings,
which also have black
tips. The female looks
very like the cabbage
whites, but her
underwings are
mottled with green.

Small Copper
May to October,
England and Wales
This little gem of a
butter-fly makes up in
beauty what it lacks in
size. Dark brownish-
grey hindwings with
an orange border,
and bright orange
forewings spotted with
brownish grey.

Holly Blue
April/May and July/
September, England and
Wales
A tiny blue butterfly,
often seen fluttering
high against a
climbing shrub.
Powder blue above,
with black wing tips,
and tiny black spots
on pale blue below.
Two broods, one in
spring and the other
in summer. Most
likely blue butterfly to
be found in gardens.

Common Blue
June to September,
almost anywhere
Male is a small-to-
medium-sized,
deep blue butterfly,
noticeably larger
than the holly blue.
White edges to the
wings. Female much
browner, with hints
of bluish above.

Speckled Wood
April/May to August/September, mainly in the south
A mainly dark brown butterfly with creamy spots on the forewings and a
row of 'eyes' along the hindwings. Mainly lives in woods, but now on
the increase and often seen in gardens, especially those with hedgerows.

Make a bark rubbing

This is a good way to appreciate the patterns made by the bark of a tree, and can also be used to identify different kinds of tree — though it's often easier to look at the leaves and the general shape of the tree to tell what it is.

bark rubbing of London plane

What to do

- Place a piece of plain white paper up against the bark of a large, mature tree.
- Using a pencil or crayon, rub firmly and evenly across the surface of the paper so that the pattern of the bark is revealed.
- Once you've made several different bark rubbings, lay them side by side so you can compare the different patterns made by different kinds of tree.

Tip

By using a large roll of plain white lining paper (which you can get from your local DIY store), you can make a continuous bark rubbing using different coloured crayons, which you can then use to wrap birthday and Christmas presents.

How to identify ...
trees

Our grandparents' and great-grandparents' generation could put
a name to most of the trees they would see in the countryside; but
in the past few decades we seem to have lost this rich store of
knowledge. Many people today walk through a wood unable to tell
which trees they're passing; which is a pity, because once you can
put a name to a tree you can also learn a lot more about it and the
wild creatures that depend on it.

To identify which tree you're looking at, it's best to use a range
of different features. For some, like the oak and horse chestnut,
the leaves are really distinctive; while for others, like the beech, the
overall shape of the tree also helps you. Buds, seeds and fruits, and
the bark are also good ways of telling one tree from another.

How to identify ...
trees

Oak

One of the best known of our native trees: large and long-lived, with a characteristic 'bushy' shape due to twisted branches. Leaves are quite long with irregular edges known as 'lobes'. In autumn, look out for acorns.

Beech

Another much-loved native tree: often very tall, with a smooth, grey trunk. Branches start quite high up, and leaves are so dense the forest floor is often clear because very little can grow beneath the canopy. In autumn, look for the tree's nuts, known as 'beechmast', which come in spiny cases.

Ash

A tall, grey tree with slender branches giving an 'open' appearance. Look out for leaves appearing in pairs along a stem, sticky black buds in spring and bunches of 'keys' (the wind-blown seeds) which appear in autumn.

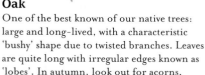

Horse Chestnut

The tree we all know and love for the fruit it provides every autumn: conkers. Leaves are very distinctive, divided into six or seven separate parts. In spring, the flowers appear in showy whitish-pink bunches; then, in early autumn, come the conkers in their green prickly cases.

Sweet Chestnut

Famous for its edible and very tasty fruit – the nuts that appear every autumn. The tree itself is quite tall and slim, with dark brown bark. The long leaves have jagged edges. Nuts come in a case with small, dense spines.

Elm

Much rarer now because of Dutch elm disease, which killed off virtually all mature trees. May still be seen as young trees in hedgerows: look for oval leaves with jagged edges.

Sycamore

A common and widespread tree, introduced here many centuries ago from southern Europe. Has large, distinctive leaves, which are divided into five parts, and very dense foliage. Tall, with a rounded outline. In autumn, look out for the 'winged' fruits which are spread by the wind.

Lime

One of our tallest and most impressive trees, with distinctive heart-shaped leaves and fat, juicy buds. Often planted in city streets and parks, as it is tough and long-lived.

Willow

The 'weeping willow' is one of our most familiar trees, with slender, golden-yellow twigs and pale green leaves hanging down in bunches, almost reaching the ground. Yellow, drooping catkins appear in spring. Usually found near water.

Silver Birch

Best identified by the pale, silvery-white bark that gives the tree its name, and peels away easily to reveal the dark wood beneath. Tall and slender, with drooping branches and leaves, and catkins in winter and early spring. Often found near water.

Norway Spruce

The classic 'Christmas tree', though if left can grow much larger than the one in your front room! Tall, slender and often triangular in shape, with long shoots covered with the short, slender needles.

Scots Pine

Our largest native conifer, widespread in Scotland but has also been planted in many other locations. Very tall and majestic, with reddish-brown bark and distinctive 'needles' (in fact, these are leaves which have adapted to retain water all year round). Produces pine cones – each segment protecting a tiny, wafer-thin seed.

Alder

Almost always found by water, this medium-sized tree has rather irregu-lar oval-shaped leaves, and produces long, drooping catkins in early spring, as well as small, black cones.

Play Poohsticks

Fans of A. A. Milne's Winnie-the-Pooh books will already be
familiar with this delightful game, which is easy to play and great
fun. You can do it on any bridge over a stream or small river – just
so long as the water flows underneath.

The rules are simple: each player finds a stick about a foot or
so long; then you all drop your sticks, at the same time, on the
upstream side of the bridge; and run over to the other side to see
whose stick comes through first.

*The game of Poohsticks first appeared in the book House at Pooh Corner, published in
1928 – though children have been playing similar games for centuries. The annual
World Poohsticks Championship is held in late March at Days Lock, Little Wittenham,
in Oxfordshire.*

Go beachcombing along the tideline

One of the most satisfying and enjoyable things you can do along
our coasts is to go beachcombing: taking a walk along the tideline
to see what you can find. Of course you can do this at any time of
year, but there's something special about being out in the middle
of winter, when the summer-holiday crowds have long gone, and
the beach is deserted.

Almost anything found at sea can eventually wash up on the
tideline, and over the course of time, much of it does. This may
be natural objects such as seashells, the bodies of dead birds or
other sea creatures, or man-made objects such as remains from
a shipwreck – or, more likely nowadays, the ever increasing
mountain of rubbish that gets dumped at sea.

So although you may occasionally come across something you
would rather not see, beachcombing is endlessly unpredictable and

fascinating, as you really do never know quite what you'll come across, even if you walk along the same stretch of tideline every day of your life.

The best time to go beachcombing is on a falling tide, as the seas reveal their secrets. Every tide brings new objects – the 'flotsam and jetsam' of the modern world. Flotsam and jetsam are used interchangeably to describe anything washed up on the beach – although strictly speaking flotsam is any object that floats (e.g. something washed off a ship or shipwreck), while jetsam is an object that has been deliberately thrown overboard by the crew of a boat or ship.

Below are some natural objects to look out for and collect.

- Pebbles: everything from rounded ones made smooth by aeons of being beaten by the waves, to sharp, jagged lumps of rock recently broken off the cliffs by autumn gales.
- Sea shells: from common-or-garden cockles, mussels, winkles and whelks, to the more exotic-looking razor shells and scallops.
- Cuttlefish bones: glowing white among the sand or shingle, these are also a common find, as are 'mermaid's purses', the egg cases of the ray or dogfish (a relative of the shark).

- Seaweed: great strands of kelp, some many metres long; or bladder-wrack, a brownish-green seaweed usually found on rocks, whose air chambers make a satisfying sound when you squeeze them between your finger and thumb until they pop.
- Fossils: depending where you are in the country, there's a good chance of finding ancient fossils – some of them many tens, even hundreds, of millions of years old.
- Driftwood: not strictly natural, as it may well be a piece of decking or other wood from a ship. But the effect of the sea will often create a really beautiful object you can take home and use as the basis for a work of art.
- Semi-precious stones: lumps of amber (fossilised pine resin about 40 million years old), or smaller, colourful gems.
- Live creatures: stranded jellyfish are common, especially after winter storms.

Some tips

- Don't go beachcombing on a rising tide – you may get cut off as the water comes up the beach.
- Wear shoes with grips such as trainers or walking boots – rocks can be very slippery.
- Turn over rocks to look for what's underneath; but make sure you put the rock back in the same place afterwards.
- Check out the tideline itself, as well as rock pools.
- Dig down into the sand to see what you can find.
- Take a bucket which you can fill with seawater to look at any living creatures you find.
- Once you've finished looking, put live creatures back where you found them – the next tide will usually wash them back to sea.
- Be careful near the underside of cliffs – rocks frequently fall, especially in winter.

How to identify ...

ducks and other waterbirds

We all love feeding the ducks, and it's another way to get to know a range of different birds. Your local park pond is a good place to start; or visit a river or lake — any large area of water will be home to a good range of the birds featured here.

Most ducks come in two plumages: male and female. The male is usually brightly coloured, and the female duller — because she does all the incubating duties, and needs to be camouflaged to avoid being seen by a hungry fox.

But ducks aren't the only waterbirds you're likely to see. Swans and geese are pretty obvious, but what about those little black birds with the white bill, or that one with red on its beak and a white streak along its side? Not ducks, but coot and moorhen, members of the rail family. Other waterbirds you may see are grebes, herons and — in much of southern Britain — egrets. If you're really lucky, a kingfisher may even flash past ...

By the way, park ponds and lakes are often home to exotic, introduced wildfowl which may not be featured in your bird book. If you're not sure what bird you're looking at, take a photo and then check it out when you're back at home using a more comprehensive bird book or the Internet.

How to identify ...
ducks and
other waterbirds

Shoveler

Male has bright green head, white breast and chestnut sides – and that huge, spoon-shaped bill which it uses to filter tiny items of food from the water. Female speckled brown like mallard, but also has huge bill.

Mallard

The classic duck – male has bottle-green head, magenta breast and white collar; female speckled brown with purplish patch on the wing. Both have yellow bills. Beware domesticated duck breeds, originally descended from mallards, that come in all shapes, sizes and colours.

Wigeon

The male is a really handsome duck: mainly grey, but with a chestnut head, creamy forehead and black under the tail. Female deep chestnut brown. Both have short, stubby bills for grazing on grass.

Gadwall

Male is subtle shades of grey, black and brown; female like female mallard but smaller. Both have small white patch on wings.

Pochard

Male has chestnut head, black breast and grey body; the female is duller and greyer, with brown head. Dives for food.

Tufted Duck

Male black with contrasting white sides, and with little black tuft on the back of his head. Female dark brown with paler sides and smaller tuft. Dives for food.

Coot

All black, apart from prominent white bill and white forehead. Larger than closely related moorhen. Chicks have red on head – easily confused with baby moorhens. Dives for food.

Great Crested Grebe

Slim, elegant bird, often seen diving for food. In spring and summer has beautiful orange and brown crests on either side of its head. In winter plainer, with white front and brown back.

Moorhen

Smaller and more slender than coot, and more colourful: with purplish-brown plumage, a jagged pale line along the sides and white under the tail. Most obvious difference from coot is the red and yellow bill.

Little Grebe or Dabchick

Tiny little bird, looking a bit like a baby duck. Fluffy rear end and short, sharp bill. In summer has chestnut patches on face.

Mute Swan

Our largest bird — elegant, serene and unmistakable. Males have slightly larger 'knob' on top of their orange bill.

Canada Goose

Big, noisy quarrelsome bird. Mainly brown, with dark neck and head and obvious white patch under the chin.

Grey Heron

Tall, slender bird with very long legs. Basically grey above and white below, with black on head and down front. Long, pointed yellow bill, ideal for spearing fish. Shy, and often seen in flight — looks huge on bowed wings.

Kingfisher

Stunning jewel of a bird: electric blue above, deep orange below, with a dagger-like bill. Much smaller than you might think — only just bigger than a sparrow.

Little Egret

Beautiful white creature — smaller than heron but similar shape and posture. Once very rare, but now doing well in southern Britain, and spreading northwards.

Spring weather lore

'March winds and April showers' pretty much sums up the British spring, but our ancestors found plenty to disagree about when it came to using nature to forecast this season's weather.

Starting with the period of fasting known as Lent, which runs for forty days from Ash Wednesday to Good Friday, it was said that:

'Wherever the wind lies on Ash Wednesday, it continues during all Lent.'

At the end of the Lent period, a similar forecast was made:

'Rain on Good Friday foreshadows a fruitful year.'

But another proverb is more ambiguous:

'A good deal of rain upon Easter Day, gives a good crop of grass, but little good hay.'

It's hardly surprising that May Day – the main celebration of the coming of spring – gave rise to all sorts of sayings which try to forecast the weather for the season ahead. Several proverbs suggest that cold weather on May Day will bring a good harvest; while the late flowering of the blackthorn (indicating a cold spring) is supposed to be good news for farmers as well. This may well be true: after all, cold winters help to kill off moulds, pests and diseases – increasing the chances of a bumper crop.

Later in the month, fine weather is hoped for – as shown by another ancient proverb:

'A swarm of bees in May is worth a load of hay.'

But perhaps the best-known spring-weather saying is meant to help us forecast the weather for the summer to come:

'Oak before ash, we're in for a splash; Ash before oak, we're in for a soak.'

This ancient rhyme suggests that if the oak tree comes into leaf before the ash, the summer will be dry; whereas if the ash is the first, a wet summer will follow.

The accuracy of this is open to debate – but what we do know is that the oak, which has generally come into leaf a few days before the ash, is now doing so much earlier than it used to, apparently as a result of climate change.

So if global warming continues to raise spring temperatures, it is increasingly unlikely that we shall ever see the ash coming into leaf before the oak again – which, according to the proverb, means summers will get hotter and drier.

Summer weather lore

St Swithun's Day – July 15 – is surely the best-known date in the weather calendar. As the old rhyme says:

St Swithun's Day if it do rain,
For forty days it will remain;
St Swithun's Day if it be fair,
For forty days will rain no more.

It's a nice idea – but does it work? Well, generally, no. Even in the wettest summer on record, 2007, there was the occasional fine day in the forty-day period after St Swithun's Day. But in the long hot summer of 1976 there were parts of southern England where it did not rain at all from the Whitsun bank holiday at the end of May to the August one: about ninety days.

The reason our ancestors needed proverbs like that of St Swithun to predict the summer weather was because they didn't have any proper weather forecasters, so had to rely on a mixture of folklore and old wives' tales. This was a particularly crucial time of year because of the annual harvest, which if it failed could lead to starvation the following winter.

So most people looked forward to the period known as the 'dog days', which begins in early July and ends in mid-August. This relates to the appearance at dawn of the brightest star in the heavens, Sirius, which is supposed to coincide with a spell of calm, settled weather.

People also used observations of natural events, and the behaviour of birds in particular, to help them forecast the weather. The habits of swallows were especially important, and gave rise to a well-known proverb:

Swallows high, staying dry;
Swallows low, wet will blow.

This has a real basis in fact. Watch swallows, house martins or swifts on a fine summer's evening, as they hawk for insects in a darkening sky. The reason the birds are flying so high is that the insects on which they are feeding are carried up into the warm, settled air by thermal currents.

On the other hand, if the birds are flying low, it is because the air currents are being disturbed, keeping the insects low too; and this usually signals a change to cooler, less settled weather.

So next time you see these graceful birds hunting for insects at dusk, check out where they're flying, and see what the weather is like the next day …